Will You Make It?

How To Create Wealth, Protect Your Lifestyle
and Plan for A Worry Free Retirement.

Martin Speiser B.Com. CA. CPF

www.willyoumakeit.com.au

Contents

Foreword

Every now and then we meet or discover a special someone who envelopes passion and pride into whatever they do. Someone whose level of expertise is matched only by their desire and dedication to help others succeed.

This book is a how to, with a parable intertwined, a real life story of one of the many clients the author has nurtured and turned their lives around with positive guidance and skill.

Written with a deep commitment to his chosen field, Martin has succinctly compiled lessons of how to achieve financial freedom. The how to of investing in Australian property, creating and protecting nest eggs, pitfalls and how to avoid them.

"Will You Make It?" provides both novices and experienced investors alike the tools and insights on how to improve their financial situations, take responsibility, learn and the value of seeking information from mentors and industry experts.

A valuable read from a trusted source. Poignant, enjoyable, informative, concisely written with a commitment to the reader's success, hats off on a remarkable book, it's a must read for anyone wanting to achieve financial freedom.

Jackie Frank
Editor
Marie Claire

About the Author

Martin Speiser has burning desire to ensure all Australians build wealth for their future and protect themselves through wise insurance and asset protection that they can afford, his legacy is his new book "Will You Make It?"

Born in Sydney, his father from Czech Republic and Mother from England, Martin still lives in Sydney with his wife and 3 children. An avid sports fan particularly Rugby League, AFL, Cricket and Basketball. Martin's other interest is collecting wine and boasts a cellar with over 700 bottles.

At 14 Martin travelled to America and was inspired by his cousin, an accountant, with a high regard for money, Martin naturally gravitated into business and finance and in 1986 graduated with a commerce degree from University of New South Wales.

Quickly landing a job with Arthur Young now industry giant Ernst & Young and completing his final year to become a Chartered Accountant in 1989.

He soon realised his passion was to help clients create wealth rather than just reporting it, and so in 1992 he embarked on a career in financial planning. July 1995, MASU Group was borne in partnership with Suren Pather with an economics law background, their aim was to establish a holistic practice as at that time the industry was mainly run by insurance agents, they were focused on creating a strategic firm.

MASU Group was also one of the first practices to incorporate property as part of their client services.

Today, MASU Group has its own AFSL, Credit Licence and Real Estate Licences with over 25 Authorised Representatives in NSW, QLD and WA and soon in SA.

Martin holds a Bachelor of Commerce (B.Com.), Accounting and Finance, is a chartered accountant, licenced Real Estate agent as well as registered tax agent and certified planner.

MASU Group specialises in areas such as:

» Diploma of Mortgage Lending
» Financial Planning
» Marketing & Liaison with Product Suppliest
» Implementing Systems for Financial Planners
» Presenting Seminars on Wealth Creation
» Running Real Estate Practice as Licencee
» Supervision of 25 Proper Authority holders

Martin works in the business implementing wealth creation strategies for high nett worth individuals, companies, Mums and Dads alike. Involving asset acquisitions (direct property, shares and managed funds), tax planning, structuring finance, implementing risk management and superannuation advice.

With a no nonsense practical approach and a passion for successful client outcomes. Martin strives to break down the barriers and provide his clients with workable plans to achieve a debt free future.

Introduction

Welcome to "Will You Make it?", my efforts here represent over 25 years of experience, hard work and a swag of grateful clients and friends which have helped me to know what I know. Maybe you are one of them!

What inspired me to write this book is mainly my clients' and the mainly negative press this industry receives.

It has given me such a deep satisfaction to help all of them and now my quest is to share my knowledge and in turn help you on the road to financial freedom.

You're probably thinking "not another book on property, shares, finances and goal setting", well guess what? You're right.

I have tried to keep it light, informative and a quick read. Sometimes you might say "Martin, you've already said that!" so bear with me, repetition and learning go hand in hand!

Whilst trying to keep the KISS principle, I will also go into some detail about what's happened here in Australia with the industry - sometimes tedious stuff, what happens to our finances when we start a family and lots of tips and instructions on how to get it right.

What I also wanted to give you are a case study, I'm sure you'll relate to their journey.

My goal is to leave you with pearls of wisdom for you to start, continue and improve your financial position and for the long term, reach YOUR retirement dream.

After all it's never too late, nor too early!

Please register this book at www.willyoumakeit.com.au to receive complimentary access to the bonus videos and worksheets that covers our initial discussions with my clients. I go over how to plan for your retirement and how to invest for your future in this interactive session.

Please enjoy.
Yours sincerely,
Martin Speiser B.Com CA CFP

What More Help Planning Your Future?

For Free Instant Access to my Financial Membership Site that has a video walkthrough showcasing a typical financial situation. Let us help you plan for a worry free retirement.

Visit my website:
www.willyoumakeit.com.au

CHAPTER ONE

The Clock is Ticking

The Clock is Ticking

"You never want to have that ticking clock and know that you had all this time and didn't use it."

J. J. Abrams

In this chapter what I do want to emphasize is whatever age you are - the clock still ticks. Planning for your future is something you need to think about at any age, and the earlier you start the better!

For this exercise we are going to hypothetically concur we are all paid monthly, so that's twelve times a year, right? If you know your twelve times tables this could be a very scary thought.

We all know what happens to our income, it seeming, simply disappears. What I want to teach you is how to make the most of it, how to get the life you want and deserve.

Some of you are well on the way, this book will also talk to you. Some of you are just starting out and feel as though you have plenty of time, this book will talk to you. And then for some of you, the clock is really ticking, with only a handful of pay days left, this book will talk to you.

Whatever category you fall into there are considerations you need to ask yourself, you need to be blatantly honest with yourself too, refer to the worksheets available from our website www.willyoumakeit. com.au and complete them, here are just a few;

» Money in, money out, what's your budget and how much do you have left from each pay?
» If you have children, what provisions do you make, need to make and just how long will they be on your hands financially?
» Lifestyle choices, do you want to travel, buy a new car, renovate your kitchen or bathroom?
» How much do you owe?
» How much are your assets worth?
» What age do you want to retire?
» How much money will you need to fund your retirement?

You may know the answers to these questions, if you don't I can help you, big time. If you do know some of the answers, this book will give you some new ideas or just jog your memory.

There may even be other questions that spring to mind, my goal is to get you thinking and take action now.

Speaking of taking action, I recently caught up again with Alex and Josie it had been quite some time!

Alex and Josie: Times and Situations Change

Alex and Josie are a middle aged couple and asked me how much money do they need to retire on and how do they best achieve it? They are planning on retiring when Alex reaches sixty. Now both well into their forties, they now also have two children.

Times have changed, having sold their investment property some years ago to build an extension to their home and pay for private schooling for the children. They felt like time was running out and somehow they were off track.

I really wanted to find them a solution on how they're going to get there, given where they are now and what they can do in terms of reaching their goals.

As the years go by, and the children grow up, priorities change. If they're going to retire at age 60, that is 240 more monthly pay packets. A scary thought!

Let's pretend now are both 60, sitting here in my office, and they're not working anymore, but they're healthy and want to go on with a nice life.

What do most people do? What would you be doing at that age? Let's see what Josie had to say when I asked her what she wanted to do in retirement:

Josie: "I would like to travel as much as I can. Go out for dinner, movies, relax and enjoy my life. Just enjoy my life".

As you can see, Josie is like most people. Basically, what they want to do is travel, enjoy their hobbies, their lifestyle. Now, in their situation, they have got children who are now ten and twelve, they'll be mid-twenties when their parents retire.

You never know, even the youngest one still might be on their hands at retirement! As you know this is the trend in the new millennium.

Generally there are two types of people. The first type would say, "Well, I'll get my children to adulthood, then they're on their own. I'll give them a good education, I'll look after them, but then they're on their own".

The second type would say, "I want to be there to help my children out and maybe help them buy a house." Buying property is expensive in Australia and the cost of living is particularly expensive in the major cities.

What type of category do you think Josie and Alex fall into?

Did you answer the Second category? Well, you'd be right!

What most people want to do is to be there to support their family, which is very important. At the moment, Alex is earning $80,000 a year, and Josie's earning $60,000.

I encouraged them to role play, imagining sitting in front of me, both now 60, and not working anymore, I then said that I'm going to be their new boss.

I said you're now going to come to me and ask for a salary, and that salary is going to allow you to do all these things. Things like go overseas maybe once or twice a year, go to the movies, restaurants, and pay for medical bills which will start getting expensive as you age.

Also you want to look after your kids and help them out. In today's dollars, because we know what a dollar's worth, what type of salary do you think you're going to need to be on?

And assuming you'd be paying tax, because we all pay tax, even if we work or don't work. What type of salary in today's dollars do you think you're going to need to be on, just to sustain that type of living? You'd say about $60,000, right?

At this point Josie agreed with me on the $60,000, though she did give me some strange looks. Now I was only kidding.

As your financial planner I'm really not going to be your employer when you're 60, so if you're not earning that income from work, where are you going to get it from? That's right, your assets. The penny dropped, Josie now was getting me. So, let's have a look.

Now as we know they were not strangers to property, but I felt they really needed a refresher course. So I began, there's only one place we're going to get our income from when we don't work, and that's from assets.

We know there's three types of assets that can give us an income stream. What are they? Number one is property. Number two is shares.

And number three, well it's not really an asset, because it devalues over time. But we need it for what's called liquidity, we need to pay for things like food, movie tickets and holidays – and it's called cash.

If we're not working, there's only really three forms of assets that can give us an income stream. Now, what we want is to preserve our capital. We don't want to lose it and run out of money.

What type of percentage return do you think assets give us, across the board? Whether it is dividends on shares, interest on cash or nett return on rents.

It's quite low, even over time, and for our exercise we will assume 5% though it could be more or less depending on which asset we select.

Now, Josie said she needed an income stream of $60 000 to create her and Alex's lifestyle and maintain it.

So, if assets are returning us 5%, how much in assets do we actually need to generate that $60,000? How good's your maths? Well that's right. We need to times it by 20.

So, if somebody wanted to retire on $60,000, we'd need 1.2 million dollars in either property, shares or cash - and that's in today's dollars.

The scary thing is, if we say that money doubles every 10 years, 1.2 million dollars today will be equal to 2.4 million in 10 years, and 4.8 million dollars in tomorrow's dollars at retirement time.

This may seem insurmountable. So now all we have to do is achieve the assets we need. Well how are you going to go about achieving those assets?

Alex and Josie: The Importance of Assets

Firstly, let's look at your major assets. Your biggest asset at the moment is your house. Right? Not really! What actually pays for the house?

That's right, you. So in fact your ability to earn an income is your biggest asset! Without that continuing, nothing's going to happen.

Josie and Alex's home is now worth one million dollars, and there's a $400,000 debt on it. They also have superannuation, combined, of around $100,000. Cash of about $20,000. And they also have a small share portfolio of $10,000.

As we analyse their position, out of these assets, what's the one asset we can't really include, in terms of our retirement assets? What asset can't give us an income stream out of this? That's right, the house.

Unless you want to start renting out rooms or you're forced to sell the house, just to sustain yourself, it doesn't provide income. If you look at the numbers carefully there is strong argument for buying a home.

Instead we could be better off renting & buying investment properties, giving us tax & rental. However, this is a minority views the good Australian is to own one's own house so for   purposes I won't this again .

So in reality, what most of us do is spend most of our working lives paying off a home only to find out that when we retire we can't afford to live in.

Your lifestyle changes or, if you don't have enough income, you may have to sell the home. Unfortunately, what most people have - their biggest asset - at the end of the day can't be used to generate income, so we need to take this out of the equation!

This can be a very emotional time. They have to be funding the mortgage for the next however many years but if we analyse their position, in terms of investment assets, they only have $130,000. They actually need 1.2 million extra dollars in assets. How are they going to do it?

This can be a very emotional time. It would be great to have the choice wouldn't it? If we analyse their position, in terms of investment assets, they have $130,000. So they have got to be funding the mortgage for the next however many years. They actually need 1.2 million extra dollars in assets. How are they going to do it?

I take this moment to stop the story and ask, what are you thinking? If this reminds you of your situation, it is certainly time for change.

Okay, so even before we get there, what we are going to be doing over the next 240 months to even give us a chance.

If I'm going to analyse any financial position - let's have a look at where most of your money is going. At the moment, like most of us, your money's going where?

Paying off a mortgage, educating your children, paying for your lifestyle - but what's your biggest expense, as a percentage of your income?

It's higher than your mortgage. You don't see it, because it gets deducted every pay period. Well, it's actually called income tax!

That's right your biggest expense is tax.

What we actually find, and it's a funny thing to say to people who are actually paying off a house, raising their children. In Australia, "the lucky country", this is known as the ""poverty trap".

It can be explained this way: Historically, from the age of 35 to when we retire, this is the age where we're going to earn most of our money.

Josie and Alex are pretty much right in the peak of all of that. But when we're earning the most of our money, where does most of our money go? It evaporates into paying our mortgage, education, lifestyle and tax. I bet you're having an "ah-ha" moment now!

If we keep paying all of that, how much of this is actually going towards building up your assets? Very little. The only thing that's actually really going towards building up your assets at the moment is mandatory superannuation.

So why it's called the poverty trap is that most people spend all their working lives paying off a mortgage and living day to day.

They get to age 60, their house is paid off and the kids are off their hands. But what have they actually done towards building up that all important asset base? Virtually nothing.

 So, they find themselves in a position where they spent all their working lives paying off a house, which more often than not - they can't afford to live in once they've paid it off.

So, what do we need to start doing now? How do we actually take this worrying situation and turn it into our asset goal?

The answer is quite obvious. We know there's only three ways, or three types of assets that can generate income down the track. In fact there's really only two because cash really isn't an asset. So how do we now create those assets? Well, the first way is property.

Do you understand how negative gearing works ? What I'll do is give you a brief explanation of negative gearing. Let's work on a $500,000 property. Generally we will assume a rental of 4%, which is $20,000 a year.

You'll have expenses like rates, taxes, body corporate, strata fees, repairs and maintenance. I'd estimate you would look at about $6,000 a year in costs, which is $14,000 in what we call net income.

Now, assuming you borrowed the entire amount, and let's assume interest rates stay around 7%, we would have an interest bill of $35,000. That would give us a $21,000 loss.

On an average tax rate, that would end up being a tax saving of around $7,000. Therefore, the real after tax cost of funding this property would be $14,000 PA or $1,166 per month.

So, if you have that per month spare that you have been putting in savings, you could generally go buy a $500,000 property. That's the old way of doing it.

What we as financial planners like to show our clients is a new way, and that is buying brand new properties, as they attract what's called non-cash deductions.

For you to get a tax deduction (and tax is a very significant part of your expenditure), you have to put your hands in your pocket. For example, you pay money for a donation, you get a tax deduction.

For home office expenses like electricity, you get a deduction. The secret of buying successful assets is to get a tax deduction just by virtue of holding that particular asset.

Let me explain it this way. Let's assume in our situation we now have a $500,000 property. It's new. Let's even assume you're going to have the same rent and same expenses as an older property.

Generally, you're going to get better rent and less expenses on the new property. But for our purposes, we'll assume it's consistent.

We'll assume the same interest rate too. The difference now, is with a new property, we get two very nice extra tax deductions. We get what's called plant and equipment depreciation, where you can write off the fixtures and fittings of this property.

For example, carpets, stoves, air-conditioning, blinds, share of common property. This could be as high as $10,000. Most attractively with a new build or new building, we also get an investment allowance, where the cost of construction can be written off over 40 years, or 2.5%.

This means, every year, we're getting tax deductions, just by virtue of holding that particular asset.

In this case, we're now going to get a conservative $12,000 depreciation allowance.

As a result, when we actually come to do our tax return, we're going to show a $22,000 tax loss for the year for depreciation and the investment allowance. Combined with our above deductions, our total loss to claim is now $43,000.

This is a tax benefit now of around $13,000. We still have the same cash outflow, but we've now got bigger tax savings. This means our real after tax cost is now going to be only $1,000 PA, which actually comes to around $83 per month.

Much less than our previous scenario above. This now becomes quite affordable, or a lot more affordable for the same type of property. This displays some of the benefits of negative gearing, I'll also cover it later in this book.

Just because it's new doesn't mean it's good. You've still got to maintain the same principles of investing in property. Buy in the right areas, have the right builders, have the right number of apartments.

The same property fundamentals apply, but if we can structure it correctly, well - we're going to need a lot less cash to fund it.

Exciting isn't it. What's going to happen is that the property's being funded by the tenants and your savings in tax.

This is a great example of how a qualified financial planner can give you robust, sound and real financial advice.

Not just an opinion, like a real estate agent, or a property spruiker selling units off the plan or something similar. Josie's sat up tall, and I could tell, hope had entered the room. This is a major benefit in my business, it really is selling hope.

What More Help Planning Your Future?

For Free Instant Access to my Financial Membership Site that has a video walkthrough showcasing a typical financial situation. Let us help you plan for a worry free retirement.

Visit my website:
www.willyoumakeit.com.au

CHAPTER TWO

6 Steps to Financial Freedom

6 Steps to Financial Freedom

"Financial freedom is available to those who learn about it and work for it."

Robert Kiyosaki

If you want to be financially free then like any goal there are always key steps to achieving them. I always show my clients my 6 key steps they should follow in order to ensure they retire worry free.

The 6 key steps are:

1. Concepts
2. Planning
3. Products
4. Implementation
5. Record Keeping
6. Review

Step 1 - Concepts:

This is all about what you think is right, your ideas — it's totally individual. Take the time to write down all your thoughts.

You may have some misconceptions, however the real benefit you'll receive is from learning your questions; only then you will get the right answers. Sounds a bit new age for sure, but guess what — it actually works!

Step 2 - Planning

Let's go back to Chapter One, where you made the list on what you want and what you need? This is a critical stage, it gives you the realisation of your current position whilst also projecting what the future may hold. Let's face it — none of us really know this!

Just one thing on planning though, Alan Lakein famously quoted "failing to plan, is planning to fail" and if you are a scuba diver you may know "plan the dive and dive the plan".

Step 3 - Products:

This is what's available to you to invest into. Whether it be property, managed funds, self-managed superannuation, bonds, cash or shares, you need to know what's available.

Now, I don't blame you if you think it's confusing, I am just going to touch on a few options here but will discuss them in detail in Chapter Four. Of course you are probably aware of all of them, what this book will give you is understanding of just how they work, you may even add them to your concepts worksheet.

The core products are:

- » Shares
- » Superannuation including Self-Managed Superannuation
- » Property
- » Managed Funds
- » Cash

It's wise to spend some time on researching these core products to help you understand them.

Shares for example could be ideal for some investors but others don't even consider them through lack of knowledge. The more facts you know about all the core products the broader your investment potential.

Step 4 - Implementation:

This is your "how are you going to do it?". Will it provide the desired outcome?

This is all about orchestration, how it will work best for you with considerations such as timing, value of your investment, if the clock's really ticking - your best option could indeed vary. I'll cover this in the next chapter on Getting the Right Advice, here's a saying I enjoy

"The best advice I ever got was that knowledge is power and to keep reading". David Bailey.

Step 5 - Record Keeping:

Whether it's your accounting or your accountant, good record keeping is the key to success, and certainly makes life easy.

It's incredibly important to have a system, particularly if property or shares is your investment choice.

Good recording keeping will save you time and a great deal of frustration, especially at tax time. The onus is on you.

Without a receipt the ATO (Australian Taxation Office) will not accept your deduction, so keep all your receipts filed. It's a great use of time to also scan and save a digital copy. It will make lodging your income tax return a breeze and, with everything kept in order, you'll save money on accountant's fees too — now that's an incentive!

Step 6 - Review:

It might sound odd, but as you know circumstances change, it's vital you keep your chosen investments up to date with your circumstances. Additionally keep abreast of new products and legislation such as tax so you remain advantaged.

One important thing most people forget, especially when caught up in changing times, is to review their situation. Whether it be a personal change or a legislation change it's just so important to know your own business and act quickly. Otherwise it could cost you dearly.

The following chapters will explain in detail just how to get your retirement goal on track.

What More Help Planning Your Future?

For Free Instant Access to my Financial Membership Site that has a video walkthrough showcasing a typical financial situation. Let us help you plan for a worry free retirement.

Visit my website:
www.willyoumakeit.com.au

CHAPTER THREE

Getting the Right Advice

It's essential and important - getting the right advice to suit your circumstances. So read on to get a better understanding about "getting that right advice".

Getting the Right Advice

"The secret of getting ahead is getting started."

Mark Twain

Financial Planning as a Solution

Have you ever thought about utilising the services of a financial planner? One of their key benefits and focus is they will help you to set goals, empower you with knowledge to make informed decisions to suit YOUR situation, that's the benefit! Sound good?

You may not think you need one, I hear you say, but I know you want the best for you, knowledge is king, so what's the harm in at least checking out your options? Yes, you guessed it, that's what I do!

Another good reason for appointing a financial planner? They are bound by codes of professional conduct and they are abreast of all legislation changes, providing you with current information.

Can you imagine keeping up with legislation changes alone?

Usually the first consultation is free, so you have absolutely nothing to lose! By engaging a financial planner to help with your situation, you will fast track the information flow, translate your options, eliminate jargon and help you on the path to have confidence in the possibilities of just how achievable financial security is.

One of the big issues we face today in this sector is that a lot of people can call themselves "Financial Planners". So how do you find the right one for you?

In this chapter, I want to dispel the myths, arm you with the knowledge to understand your options and encourage you to think and be excited about your new life.

The perception in the community of most Financial Planners is I think, very, very misunderstood. It has all stemmed from many people calling themselves financial planners.

Now anyone in the old days could put up a shingle on their window saying "Mortgage Broking", "Financial Planning", or "Insurances and Financial Planning". So the community for a long time, simply didn't understand, what financial planning was all about.

In Australia the governing body over financial planners is the Financial Planning Association. Recently they have been trying to increase public awareness through advertising campaigns.

The measure of their success? Well I think the jury's still out, it will be a shame if the Mums and Dads and small investor markets miss out on this message though.

Then there's ASIC (Australian Securities & Investments Commission) who have been putting in some very harsh rules in terms of the people who can actually call themselves a financial planner of late.

Under ASIC's guidelines someone who is actually a licensed financial planner, has a dealer's license, or is an authorized representative.

An authorized representative is someone who's qualified, and who's able to receive what's called a "proper authority" from a dealer group who has an Australian Financial Services License to be able to give financial planning advice.

This is what you need to ascertain, we don't go to the butcher when we need a haircut, so it's an important message for you!

Sorry to rant, but I think it's really important, so again, when looking at financial planners, you've got to make sure of;

Number one: the financial planner actually has what's called proper authority from a dealer group.

Number two: you actually look at an Australian Financial Services license number.

Preferably the financial planner should be a member of the Financial Planning Association. This has been implemented through regulation to avoid confusion as to who is actually giving financial planning advice.

Scrutiny of accountants

In recent years financial planners have been scrutinised heavily to conform to these guidelines, and this is now in turn affecting accountants, this is in place to protect you.

A lot of people used to go to their accountants for financial planning advice, you may fall into this category, if that's you, I think it's a wise move to reassess your situation.

Accountants fall under the same regime, that they're not properly qualified if they don't have proper authority or have a dealer's license. In that case, they're not really able to give financial planning advice.

For example, if you go to your accountant and say, "Should I invest in XYZ shares?" the accountant is basically not allowed to say, "Yes, you should."

Technically what he's supposed to say is, "I recommend you see a financial planner who can actually give you the correct advice."

Unfortunately, there are still some people out there giving this type of advice unlicensed, so one does really need to be careful about who they're talking to.

Today many are people setting up their own superannuation fund and actually going to their accountant to ask A) whether they should be doing it and B) to set it up for them, I'll cover more on superannuation later in this book.

But for now the real message I want to send is to ensure that you are dealing with an accredited individual or company, that's where you'll get the best advice.

The other thing is a lot of times accountants are restricted in the kinds of advice that they can give you i.e. some of the dealer groups might let planners do a little bit of limited insurance and manage a few funds, so they actually don't have the full spectrum of advice available which leads to a kind of limited product range on offer, most of you would like a plethora of choice, I'm sure.

The best way is to be armed with questions and interview them! Remember you're paying good money for their service.

What you're actually seeing today is there are many accountants recognizing this, and either they tried to joined dealer groups, i.e. for an accountant, getting an accreditation of what's called RG146, which is getting the appropriate training to get proper authority - or - teaming up with firms of financial planners. So there is a good chance if you have an accountant that they are accredited.

Now, that is good in one respect but bad in another, because if an accountant is giving financial planning advice, are they able to give financial planning advice plus do your tax plus do all the other compliance work. It may be wise not to put all your eggs in one basket!

Don't get me wrong here, we've all got to recognize an accountant is extremely valuable, but they're there to perform a certain role. That is compile tax returns, give general tax advice, but not really the investment advice. Leave the investment advice to the professionals!

As you most likely know good advice from a professional is not usually free. One thing to remember is without it you will more than likely maintain a holding pattern and unless good fortune such a the lottery or games of chance rains on you, your situation will remain stagnant.

Just like Josie and Alex did, years with their heads in the sand, treading water, before making the leap of faith and consulting a professional, quite simply for a few dollars it turned their lives around, enriched them with knowledge and relieved them from the feeling of desperation. Is it worth it? YES!

Still unsure? Take a look at the successful people you know. What they do is surround themselves with industry experts to help them, that's one of their secrets to success.

What More Help Planning Your Future?

For Free Instant Access to my Financial Membership Site that has a video walkthrough showcasing a typical financial situation. Let us help you plan for a worry free retirement.

Visit my website:
www.willyoumakeit.com.au

CHAPTER FOUR

It's all about identifying the risk

This chapter is dedicated to understanding the risks involved, industry bodies and an overview of how the financial planning works, ethics and how you're protected.

It's all about identifying the risk

"The biggest risk is not taking any risk… In a world that changing really quickly, the only strategy that is guaranteed to fail is not taking risks."

Mark Zuckerberg

The role of ASIC & FPA

Here's a bit of the heavy stuff. I'll discuss the role of the corporate regulator, ASIC (the Australian Securities and Investments Commission) which regulates all companies throughout Australia.

In very broad terms, as far as the financial planning industry is concerned the role of ASIC is to administer the Corporations Act and its related legislation which cover the provision of financial services in Australia.

Now ASIC have come in for a lot of criticism from many quarters for the job that they are doing. It is not part of the scope of this book to go into all that but I will say that I think that the criticism that ASIC have copped for the way that they have regulated the industry is unjustified.

The task of managing the thousands of Australian Financial Services Licensees and the tens of thousands of corporate and individual Authorised Representatives that the licensees have authorised to render financial services on their behalf is a huge one.

This industry has the tendency to attract 'bad eggs' and I think that ASIC have been very quick and proactive in weeding these bad eggs out and removing them from the industry, either banning them for a few years if their misdeeds have not been of the worst type or banning them altogether and for life if they are downright dishonest and crooks.

So, whilst ASIC have come in for a lot of flak when there have been product failures or for not acting quickly enough, I think that everyone has to be realistic in their expectations of what a corporate regulator/policeman can do. The reality is that more often than not, there is little that the regulators and law enforcers can do but to come in after the event, sort out the mess and punish the wrongdoers and ASIC have no doubt been very good at that.

Conversely, when companies and individuals have made honest mistakes and have fallen short of what is required of them, ASC have been quite pragmatic and shown a willingness to allow these companies and individuals the opportunity of correcting their mistakes.

If you have been following any of the developments in this regard you will know how confusing and shambolic things can get with frequent changes in policy when governments change and even within the life of the same government. As I said though that is not a subject for this book but perhaps a subject that I will go into in another book.

Product failures

We have seen repeatedly though how seriously people's lives can be affected by bad and dishonest advice and by product failures.

There were countless product failures in the days leading up to and after the Global Financial Crisis and these failures literally and figuratively destroyed the lives of thousands. Some investors who lost everything even ended up taking their own lives.

One of the effects of all these product failures and bad advice is that there has definitely been a trend to only having the big institutions delivering financial advice. Many of the smaller operators have gone to the wall.

On the one hand having big institutions only delivering financial advice, products and services is good, because they have the resources to ensure that their financial services are delivered according to the law and if things go wrong, they are able to make good the losses that those who have received bad advice at their hands have suffered.

On the other hand, the big institutions just cannot in my view deliver the personal financial advice that so many 'mum and dad' type of investors want and need.

If you go to one of the big banks for your advice the chances of your walking away from the process with anything but the products of that bank itself are small. And that makes perfect sense. If you go to ABC bank why would they sell you products manufactured by DEF bank?

But if you wanted very particular advice on matters such investment structures or for example buying a residential property for investment purposes you will be very unlikely to get that advice from a bank. It's not what they do so they won`t be able to help you on that.

The smaller boutique dealers

So if you really can`t get the kind of advice you want and need from a big institution then you have to get your advice from one of the smaller 'boutique' type institutions.

Unfortunately, these 'boutique' operations are becoming more and more of a rarity. Many got caught up in the product failures of the mid to late 2000s and went out of business because of the claims that were made against them.

Some have argued that this is not a bad thing because the smaller operations recommended the 'toxic' products that did so much damage much more frequently than the big instos so they ended up doing serious harm to their clients.

But despite the losses that some of these smaller operator caused I still say that there is not only room for the smaller operators but it is essential that the investing and advice seeking public have the opportunity to get true financial advice from a dealer group that is free of the constraints of having to sell the products of the manufacturer of that product.

The problem for the smaller groups though is that they have to make their living out of the commissions that the product manufacturers pay them for recommending their products or out of fees that they charge their clients.

Earning commissions form product sales is a major topic of discussion and ultimately there is a bi-partisan consensus that the whole industry needs to move away from commissions to a 'fee' based remuneration model.

The problem with that approach is that very few people are ready to pay for financial advice. Certainly, it is extremely difficult to run a business based only on fee for service model and the authorities and 'powers that be' know that if they were to immediately ban all commission remuneration and legislate an overnight introduction of fee for service, the effect of that would be the virtual complete cessation of people seeking financial advice.

That would be catastrophic all round. If nothing else, the chronic under insurance situation that already exists in the life insurance area would be made much worse because virtually nobody would buy insurance if they not only had to pay the premiums for it, but also had to pay for the advice to buy it in the first place!

The net effect of that outcome would be a lot more people putting their hand out to the government for financial help when disaster strikes. No government will want that.

Finally then on this topic, can anyone who provides financial planning be called "independent"? The answer is only if they receive absolutely no commission from any product sales!

And as I have already said, there are very few of those.

Education and continuing education

It's important…………………..

CHAPTER FIVE

Why Property is an essential part of your Portfolio

Why Property is an essential part of your Portfolio

"It's tangible, it's solid, it's beautiful. It's artistic, from my standpoint, and I just love real estate."
Donald Trump

We love it, it's tangible, real estate is the favorite of most - including the investor. Real estate has been the saving grace of many mainstream investors over time, you probably know of them and of course you know Josie and Alex!

Whether it's a property portfolio within a managed fund or the typical purchase of the family home, land or units, there are questions you may have, sure some of these are easily answered by logic.

I've already talked about the accountants and their requirements and how they can't generally give financial planning advice.

Currently there's an extremely grey area in the domain of property and advice unless qualified.

Australians have a love affair with property and many Australians, if they can, will buy an investment property.

Firstly, I must confess I am a big advocate of property!

So, I am going to start with a story of some old clients of mine. You may know their story, you may have walked this walk, you may have a desire to do what they did, or you may not yet be in their position to venture this road, whoever you are, meet Alex and Josie!

About 15 years ago now this lovely young couple in their early 30's came to me for advice on what to do with a rather small windfall, they had twenty thousand dollars to invest! Certainly a lot of money for them.

Their position was they had a mortgage on their own home of $350,000, their property was valued at $500,000 (this meant they had $150,000 equity), both had good jobs and collectively they were earning around $120,000 before tax.

Their big question to me was how to maximise their windfall? They had thought of shares, superannuation and property, but were totally perplexed with media articles, parents' and friends' advice, they were totally confused and in need of help translating their new knowledge.

I was relieved to discover their preference was an investment property, as it suited their circumstances best to a tee.

The challenge now was finding the right one. Decisions like location, old versus new, determining rental returns, estimating capital growth, things like that. Their hearts were set on a renovation project on an older property.

You know I totally got them, with Alex being a builder and Josie really wanting to lend a creative hand, which we see all the time in the popular renovation series on TV, they set out in search of an investment property.

The great thing about their situation is they had equity and what this meant, is lenders would give them up to 90% of the property's value.

I explained the benefits of purchasing a new property over an existing older property, naming the benefits of a higher rental yield, less ongoing expenses and the fact they could acquire a property for around $225,000 in a high growth area (back then this is what a two bedroom Western Sydney apartment was selling for).

What we did need to do is set a budget to fall into these parameters, that being $225,000 - a toughy indeed! Finally we found an off the plan apartment in Western Sydney.

Factoring in stamp duty (at investor's rate), legal fees and other costs, the total amount was $240,000.

Long story short, on completion, it rented immediately. Two years down the track, they had a good tenant, the property returns just over $10,000 per year, the interest and rates on the property are 19,000 per year, so a loss of $9,000 each year.

However, amongst their expenses they receive approximately $29,000 in tax deductions through negative gearing, which makes this property neutral to positively geared!

Yes here's the thing; they did buy well and that's the key, most excitingly the property is now conservatively worth $550,000.

Translated they have a property that costs them nothing per week and they now have $310,000 equity in the investment.

Now that's a dream outcome, thanks to them, they had the wisdom to seek advice and the tenacity to make their own luck. I will give you an update on the couple later, you'll be surprised about life's little turns.

Buyer Beware

We've already seen the appearance over the last 10-15 years of what we call property spruikers. These are groups and companies who push investment properties all over the country on the basis that these are so-called "good investments", for their own exclusive benefit.

At the moment, there's no legislation to protect buyers in this field, because property is a state-run legislation. Most of these you would hope are real estate agents, but in fact they are not required to hold any form of investment qualification.

There's obviously a risk for the consumer here, yet nothing has been done.

Some of the larger property organizations are realizing that this could all possibly change, and they are making concerted efforts to go down the road of becoming dealer groups or getting proper authority as a licensed real estate agent.

So the big problem potential investors are facing in this area is that it's a real buyer beware market. We are talking big dollars here, I can't stress enough the importance of getting sound independent advice.

In the investment field, if something goes wrong with an investment and the advisor who recommends that investment can be shown to be negligent or not acting in the best interest of the client, the client has various avenues to get compensation, either through the financial ombudsman service, or even the courts, so the consumer is somewhat protected.

Unfortunately, with property, there is no such protection. They can go through the various channels of the Department of Fair Trading and various Real Estate Institutes, but as I said, it's a buyer beware market. So property at the moment is a very grey area in financial advice.

Technically speaking, if a purchaser of a property goes to an agent and says, "Is this a good investment?" under the current law, the agent should say, "I'm not able to give advice in this area. You should seek independent financial planning advice."

I think we all know this generally never happens. There's many real estate agents who would say, "Yes, this is a good investment. This is what you'll get as a rental. This is your rental yield, etcetera." I know you get it, you have probably experienced it, the problem is that most people take the advice in trust, and that's when problems occur.

So what do we look for when we're selecting a property? Very importantly, if it's a new property, who is the developer? Has that developer got a good reputation? Has he been in the market for a while? Because ultimately, they're going to need to be around to fix any defects or any other issues once the property is complete.

The old saying is, "Location, location, location." We've always got to bear in mind that we need to be close to the amenities, such as shops, transport, schools, and entertainment. Because if we're going to rent these properties out, that's what the tenants want to have.

I'm also very cautious about the number of units in a development. Buying in a block of 60 is not like buying in a block of 300. Because in the larger blocks, there's obviously pressure on renting them. Because if you're renting it, so are 100 other owners, which can force the rentals down.

The same with selling. If you're selling your apartment, do you want another 20 or 30 in that development also selling at any one time? That's only going to put price pressure downwards.

There is also something to be said with land value, land is the commodity that actually appreciates, so when amortised across the volume of units, it works this way: the bigger the land and smaller the complex, generally means a higher value.

But we also need to be cautious of body corporate fees. Some of the larger developments, which have pools and gyms, concierge etc. - charge high body corporate fees.

If you're relying on rental income to fund the investment property, these type of expenses can considerably reduce the rental yield.

Again, for people buying properties as an investment, I would exercise a lot of caution and I would very much urge people to contact well qualified financial planners whose focus is property to get the right type of advice in buying property.

Let me just briefly here give you some information to arm you better when you do take the step into property.

Why Australia? Well, as we all know, Australia is a very politically stable country. We don't suffer many fluctuations in our economy, and rarely in our property market. We have a pretty large economy and a skilled labour force - who earn income and need places to live - either to buy or to rent.

We have excellent educational facilities throughout the country, which not only provides a very good employment base, but also brings in a lot of overseas students and families.

We have a lack of usable land. Australia is predominantly a strip of habitable land along the Eastern seaboard. We have vast land in the middle of the country, which can't be really used for housing, or at least isn't yet. This lack of usable land creates limited supply. What the real issue at the moment is, affordability.

While house prices become unaffordable - in certain areas, it creates opportunities for investors, because people need to rent.

But what it also does do, is it flows into more affordable neighbouring areas, thereby creating a need for housing in those areas, and so forth and so on, I'm sure you've seen it.

At the moment, under the foreign investment review board, overseas buyers can buy Australian property. What this is doing is creating a healthy demand, but also creating supply and construction issues.

So why property? Well the statistics say that by the year 2061, the population of New South Wales is projected to reach 11.5 million, which is an increase of 4.2 million, or 57% from 2012.

Victoria's estimated to reach 10.3 million, an increase of 4.7 million, or 83%. And Queensland is expected to reach 9.3 million, which is an increase again of 4.7 million, or 100%.

All these people need a place to live. So the people who own property will be doing very nicely, given there's going to be such demand and limited supply.

The major market today for buying investment property is Sydney - particularly an area of around 16 to 20km from the CBD. Next comes outer Sydney, which is out beyond the CBD and near CBD suburbs.

We also have markets in Melbourne, Brisbane CBD and Brisbane regional, which includes the Gold Coast, and other areas in Australia, such as Perth, country New South Wales and Country Victoria.

Sydney continues to drive the residential property price increases. Just in the years 2013 to 2014, we've actually seen a 14.6% increase. Now some people are saying, "Well that is creating a bubble, which is about to pop."

However, after 25 years of seeing ups and downs, given the limited amount of land, the population increases - sure, we might get a drop, we might get a correction, but ultimately, I can only see one way for prices in Sydney, and that's moving upwards. The same can be said for the other major capital cities.

The big issue facing property today is a lack of supply. There's not enough land for the construction that we need to house the population increases. Another major issue - which is causing restricted supply are the banks.

They're making it extremely difficult for new developers in relation to their finance requirements which have become very tight since the global financial crisis.

This is causing a high level of pre-sales for developers. So if they want to complete a project, a construction - today they pretty much have to pre-sell their entire amount of debt before the banks will give them any finance.

The lack of land is resulting in a lack of quality sites. There's also no incentive for developers. Not only do developers today have to build, fund the holding costs, and the construction costs, the councils are making them put in hefty contributions - putting in parks, driveways, roads, utilities, also they have to pay GST, so effectively all their sales are reduced by 10%.

There's also a lack of infrastructure as a lot of the areas which require development, have no water, electricity, roads - which all have to be funded by the developers.

Now, the governments and councils know that there's a problem out there and they haven't found a solution. We're not finding a solution and we're not getting enough housing to fulfill the demand of a rising population.

Another major factor is housing affordability. House prices, particularly in Sydney, continue to increase. Which means, the first home owners are getting squeezed out of buying - which means, they're forced to rent.

This actually puts the investors in a much stronger position and those that can afford to buy property will do well.

So in summary, a rising population and lack of supply will continue to force prices up. Prices are on the rise. The lack of affordability increases demand for rental accommodation. The lack of rental supply actually forces rents higher. If we can afford property, let's buy it!

Abolition of Negative Gearing – A Fear Factor

The one issue in the back of everyone's mind in the industry is what happens if the Government removes the tax breaks associated with negative gearing? This notion rears its head from time to time, thus far it is the elephant in the room. I have a few thoughts on this.

Firstly I think this would no doubt cause a crisis in the rental market with investors no longer having an incentive to purchase property.

In turn removing a considerable amount of stock from the rental market.

If housing were to remain unaffordable to buy then where would renters find property? This would force the Government to have to provide more public housing which is a considerable drain on their funding.

Secondly if there was no demand for rental properties this could lead to a major crisis in the construction industry which could ultimately place pressure on unemployment. The construction industry has long been a barometer of Australia's viability.

This industry hires many qualified and unqualified laborers, builders, plumbers, carpenters, architects, draftsmen, engineers – the list goes on. What effect would that have then on high school graduates in their choices of further education and courses?

Thirdly, and absurdly never mentioned is the lack of revenue from not only property stamp duty (a major source of funding to the State Governments), but at the other end too with capital gains tax, I'm sure they want this to continue.

Additionally the local councils are largely funded by development applications, building permits and residential infrastructure revenue.

Fourthly, and quite cheekily, a recent survey showed a very high proportion of members of parliament negative gear and why shouldn't they?

The proponents of removing negative gearing would probably achieve their goals of an easing in price pressure on property though at what ultimate price?

The Key to Success

When people ask me, "What is the key to buying successful property?" To me, it's buy where the locals want to buy and live. I've seen so many examples of people buying in certain parts of the country.

For example, if there's a development in North Queensland, and the only people that are buying those properties are people from Sydney and Melbourne, and not the locals, it's a warning signal.

Because, if the locals don't want to buy in these projects - if the investor has to sell that property, you're going to need a local market, because these things won't be marketed to Sydney and Melbourne people once they're complete.

You'll always want to be able to rent to the locals, and sell to the locals.

In terms of property management, the key to having a successful rental property is to have a good and reliable manager. At the start, they'll go in and look at defects and help with finding good tenants.

Ensuring tenants pay the rent on time and if there are any disputes they will work to resolve them.

The maximum fees that I believe a rental property manager should charge is 5.5%. to 8.8%. Be cautious of those charging too low a fee as it's better to pay a little more and have a job well done.

Property managers usually charge the first weeks letting fee as their finder's fee, this is common practice. Don't forget though, property manager's fees are 100% tax deductible too!

A good property manager will always communicate with you. They'll let you know how things are going, when you should increase rent, provide advice on maintenance issues, provide copies of tenancy inspection reports and generally be your eye on the ground.

Our approach is to always recommend our clients to good property managers with a sound track record.

Taking the Plunge – The Mortgage

One of the first steps to buying your first property or any property for that matter is organising your finances.

A big part of this process is to determine just how much you can afford, the answer may often conflict with what you want!

Structuring your mortgage is really important, especially when it comes to investing. Firstly there's the aspect of record keeping for taxation and more importantly is the benefit to you!

When Josie and Alex first came to me I recommended the take out an "Interest Only" loan, the preferred method of most investors, this made the couples loan even more affordable for their disposable income and enabled them also to put a little away each week.

Now days the lending industry is incredibly cut throat offering fabulous rates, an interest only loan may be the best vehicle when you don't want to over commit.

Here's a summary of the loan types available to you:

Interest only

This type of loan is provided by lenders in both fixed and variable formats, basically you only repay the interest. What this means is after a year or whatever your fixed term is, you still owe the principle amount borrowed.

Things to take into account here are yield on investment, potential capital growth and intention to hold a property.

Now without the crystal ball it is difficult to predict ones future, 'Interest Only' loans can however be a handy tool, remember you can always revert to 'Principal and Interest' at a later date as long as your loan term is not fixed this can be quite a simple transition.

Principal and Interest

Here's the difference. Your repayments are more however you are actually paying back the interest and reducing the loan amount, most first home or principal place of residence loans are on this basis.

The choice of loan type is completely individual and many conservative investors will elect a P & I loan.

Interest Rates

Research can be a key indicator but I say it's still a gamble, like who can predict another GFC? Having said this there are generally times that we can predict some stability, decline or rise in rates.

How will you know this? It can be as simple as trusting in someone who deals with finance on a daily basis, someone with your best interest at heart, someone who will advise you whether fixed or variable is the right thing for you.

This choice can save you thousands in interest, trust me, it can be a paperwork jungle but it is certainly worth it, let's take a look at the options.

Variable Interest

Here the interest rate goes up or down in response to changes in the cash rate or changes by your credit provider.

Advantages of a variable rate is that interest usually goes down if the cash rate decreases, in turn reducing the amount of interest you pay.

Another positive is mostly there are no restrictions should you wish to make additional repayments or pay your loan out before the due date.

Unfortunately the opposite also applies: variable rates usually go up if the cash rate is increased, which means you will pay more interest. Here's where you need to watch the market or maybe I can do that for you!

Fixed rate

Fixed rates allow you to lock in an interest rate on your loan, typically for 1 to 5 years, in turn safeguarding you from future interest rate rises. The great thing with fixed rates is you know exactly how much you need to pay!

The downside is if rates were to fall you won't benefit. There can also be penalties on early payout of the loan, or restrictions of making additional payments. Each lender is different so it's really a good idea to spend time investigating your options.

Negotiating with Lenders

These days you are really sitting in the box seat, with so much competition out there, the banks NEED YOUR business, this makes it so important to research what's on offer, lender's products and how to play them to your advantage.

What I set up for Josie and Alex was a multiple loan amalgamation, this was such an attractive deal for the lender that they really had a great win of .05% less than the cheapest lender, this over the duration of the loan provided them with thousands of dollars, that essentially without the right research and advice they would have missed out on.

The basic rule as far as I'm concerned is that where a deductible (investment) loan exists and a non-deductible (home mortgage) loan exist and where you do intend to pay down principal then always pay off the home mortgage first.

Many people have been caught out thinking that if they pay down their home mortgage then buy another property to live in as their new home and then keep the original home as an investment that this could be a good strategy.

This defies the principal of maximising legitimate deductions and potential equity gain in your primary security, your own home.

What I mean here, is your new home, the one you are going to live in provides no tax deductions on the mortgage's interest.

Essentially you would have a non-deductible home loan and then have to pay tax on your rental income as there are no longer any deductions to offset the income.

They could well be subject to capital gains tax if they sell their first home in the future (subject to time) so ultimately this could end up being a really bad idea.

I would always suggest appropriate advice is sought before going down this path.

LVR and Self-Examination

Loan Value Ratio or LVR : Self-assessment, a quick guide to investment property affordability

Concerned about afford-ability? You are not alone and of course there is criteria that needs to be met from lenders and financial institutions.

If you have a secure validated income stream and equity in your own home, there's a good chance you will qualify for an investment loan.

Firstly you must identify your income and expenses to see just what's left over for repayments. Next you need to do a hypothetical of your situation once you've bought your property.

Stick to your budget and always include a buffer should an unexpected event arise.

There are many home loan calculators readily available on the web that will predict your repayments based on how much you need to borrow.

Financial institutions generally provide a simple formula, Loan Value Ratio or LVR, this calculation can be done at home and will give you a better understanding of just how the banks tick when assessing your risk.

At face value it's an easy calculation, here's an example assuming you have equity or a cash deposit.

Property Value $300,000 divided into the loan amount, say $220,000 for this example (so an $80,000 deposit), results in a 73.3% LVR.

Another example assuming you already own a home and want to buy a second is:

Property 1 existing home is worth	$500,000
Property 2 investment property is worth	$400,000
This would give you a total asset pool of	$900,000
Property 1 has a debt owing of	$150,000
Property 2 you want to borrow	$400,000
This gives you a total liability of	$550,000

Property Value $900,000 divided into the loan amount $550,000, results in an LVR of 61.1%.

For some of you, this may be your 'ah ha' moment, this is how property owners afford to build wealth.

Another key criteria is what the banks call serviceability, this simply means your ability to pay back the loan.

Rental income on your investment is taken into account, it can vary between lenders but usually the rule of thumb is 75%. The extra 25% makes up the difference between the gross and nett rent, the direct rent cost component.

Preparing Your Loan Application

Your financial advisor will need to see proof of a few things for the lender, if you're borrowing for the first time they like to see a savings history, all borrowers will need to show proof of income and generally the last two years tax returns & assessments and two recent pay slips and a complete list of your assets and liabilities (what you owe and what you own).

Lenders will give you a checklist of what documents they require, so get organised. Loan approval times can vary especially during holiday periods, so be sure to check with your lender what their time frames are from the initial application to finalising the contract.

If this period is exceeded you will need to ask the vendor for an extension of finance through your legal representative.

It is best to avoid this, nervous vendors may see this as a concern and reason to void the contract and maybe take a better offer waiting in the wings.

For those buying off the plan, generally banks won't or can't give a formal approval prior to exchanging. The reason is that completion may not be for several months (or years) and they recognise that circumstances may change over this period.

So if you are buying one of these properties you will have to back your ability to get finance on completion.

A few things can be done to reduce the risk. You should ensure that if completion would be today you could qualify for settlement.

A good broker can give this indication (though obviously no guarantee).

Generally the contract of sale will have a settlement clause that says settlement will be the latter of 7 days of the issue of a strata plan or occupation certificate.

I do not think this is sufficient as most banks won't do a valuation on the property till the certificates are issued and 7 or even 14 days is not enough time for them to get the loan documents ready, this then means a visit to a solicitor prior to signing.

I would always get your solicitor to request a 21 day period on the contract to avoid a lot of stress.

In short it's really important that you have good relationships with the people organizing the property and finance, that's where a financial planner is such a valuable ally who can coordinate this for you.

What about Mortgage Brokers?

Mortgage Brokers are a good option as they have access to most lenders, whether you choose to deal direct with a Bank or a broker that essentially is up to you. What you do need is a low interest rate and good service.

» Phone several - you'll quickly be able to gauge who wants your business.
» Ask for a better deal, it won't cost you anything
» Be careful of honey moon rates lower than market rates in the beginning come back to bite.

MYTH – Mortgage brokers are more expensive

Negative Gearing and Deductions

I've already touched on this, but I want to talk about how negative gearing works and how it can be possible to build a sustainable future with property in your portfolio.

If you don't understand how negative gearing works by now, just remember Josie and Alex.

Buying an Investment Property – old vs new

In chapter five I discussed some of the pit falls when buying new property, its location and the perils of property spruikers, so I am just going to keep it simple here and address the key points.

In fear of stating the obvious here, there are two major benefits;

1. Depreciation
2. Maintenance

Investment property and depreciation – The pros and cons

What is a Depreciation Schedule?

A Depreciation Schedule is a report performed by a Quantity Surveyor. It is an analysis of your property's building and plant value and an essential tool to ensure you maximise your legal taxation deductions and receive the benefit you deserve.

A Quantity Surveyor can also do reports on properties deductions. Invest in a Depreciation Schedule.

What about stamp duty and all that legal stuff?

These are known as capital expenses and are only realised when you sell the property, they do depend on your circumstance, here are a few examples:

» Stamp Duty
» Conveyance Costs (legal fees)
» Major Additions and Improvements

There is a smorgasbord of excellent information on the web for you to get up to speed and make the most of your new investment, this will give you some great questions to ask your financial planner!

How much does it cost?

Prices vary depending on a few factors like your property's size, generally they start at about $500.00 and their fee is also a tax deduction.

A Quantity Survey Report is a great investment, one that repays you each year at tax time for the duration of ownership. There''s nothing to lose and everything to gain!

What does it involve?

A Quantity Surveyor will need to inspect the property, measure and analyse each component methodically and prepare a Depreciation Schedule, this usually takes around 2 weeks.

Overview

There are two types of allowances:

Plant and Equipment – items such as dishwashers, carpets, lighting
Building Allowances – Construction costs

Note: Item 2 is only applicable to construction post 1985

The ATO (Australian Taxation Office) offers an excellent guide to
depreciation, including case studies. You can visit www.ato.gov.au
for detailed information or simply ask your financial planner.

There's also at the moment, government incentives, in terms of
stamp duty reductions and first home owner's grants - which only
apply to new properties.

Do your research, and don't miss out, a depreciation schedule
will significantly affect your bottom line. If you already have an
investment it's not too late to realise some past deductions.

Talk to your accountant as there's a good chance an amended return
may be lodged.

Buying an Investment Property

There are many considerations in buying an investment property, you no doubt by now remember Josie and Alex, with their successful venture, you probably have friends or relatives too, who've enjoyed property success

Your major costs are stamp duty, real estate commission on sale, conveyance and advertising. The sum of these costs can amount to tens of thousands of dollars, so it is critical you do your homework. It's not for the feint hearted in any aspect.

If you do succeed in making a profit there's the addition of Capital Gains Tax down the road. So it's a good reason to keep impeccable records of every dollar spent.

At the end of the journey, it is often the case to reassess selling the property, a tenant may be a better financial option, especially in a buyer's market.

Buying to Hold – medium to long term

This almost certainly involves renting the property. Good tenants are gold, to attract a high caliber tenant it's important to present your property in optimum condition, this will naturally also give you the best rental return.

Key areas to focus on whether renting or buying that attract buyers and tenants alike are kitchens and bathrooms.

Upkeep on a property can certainly eat a sizeable chunk out of your pocket and certainly needs to be factored in when buying a home.

Electrical wiring, roofing, gutters can be a huge expense for older homes, whereas a new home is built to high standards and is also covered by the builders insurance for any defects that occur under the warranty period.

Your investment property should over time appreciate in value. If you're in a high income bracket you will also enjoy the benefits of tax minimisation through negative gearing.

Your accountant is a handy resource for ensuring you optimize your legal entitlement; here are just a few of the items you can claim annually;

» Loan Interest
» Property Management Fees
» Repairs and Maintenance
» Travel to inspect your property
» Insurances
» Rates
» Depreciation

As in Josie and Alex's situation the benefit of tax deductions through negative gearing not only meant an investment property was affordable, it actually set them on the path to a comfortable retirement with their asset growing over time.

They have never looked back and now with equity in their first investment are well on track for their next investment property.

Your financial planner will advise you just what's applicable to your situation.

Selling your property - The Pointy End

Contracts and Negotiating your sale

As you read with Josie and Alex in the later years, their situation had changed. Sometimes in order to fund your retirement you need to dispose of an investment or even your own family home.

Finally they come, offers of contract.

Remember each state differs, it's important to get the facts. I'm not suggesting that you don't have a solicitor or conveyancer, they are very important!

What More Help Planning Your Future?

For Free Instant Access to my Financial Membership Site that has a video walkthrough showcasing a typical financial situation. Let us help you plan for a worry free retirement.

Visit my website:
www.willyoumakeit.com.au

CHAPTER SIX

How Do Managed Funds Work?

How Do Managed Funds Work?

"If you have some money to invest and would prefer a professional to make investment decisions for you, a managed fund might be for you."

ASIC MoneySmart

Managed funds can be a very important tool in creating wealth, particularly for those who enjoy investing in equities and commercial property. We've discussed investing in residential property, which has it's obvious advantages.

If people don't like the concept of investing in property, you can invest in the share market. Now when I say invest in the share market, generally there are I say two ways of investing in shares.

The first is what we call direct shares. This is where you go, you find a stockbroker and you go and purchase a bundle of shares. Most stockbrokers will say that you need at least $10,000 to purchase a particular share.

Now, if you have hundreds of thousands of dollars, this is good, because then we can diversify into A, different shares, B, different industries such as mining, industrial, tourism, infrastructure and so forth.

Given that most of us don't have hundreds of thousands of dollars to invest in the share market, managed funds can be a very good option. This is where we give our money to a fund manager. These guys are usually owned by banks or large institutions.

They employ analysts, technical researchers and brokers and they take our money and they pool it with hundreds of millions of dollars, maybe even billions of dollars of other funds.

They can then go and buy meaningful quantities of shares in many companies and in many industries, which actually gives us a good form of diversification.

For example, we might have say $20,000 to invest. We can split that $20,000 into various asset classes such as, fixed interest, Australian shares, international shares, infrastructure, commodities and so forth.

This can also be tax effective as if they're invested in the share market, we get imputation or Franking credits, which can be used to offset our tax.

If they're invested in commercial properties, we can get property credits, just like depreciation and building allowances. These can be very tax effective as well.

I generally encourage my clients who have spare capacity to use this form of investment and it also can be used very effectively with a concept called "dollar cost averaging".

This is where we put in money on a regular basis. What this does is iron out any fluctuations in the market.

Let's just say for an example, we're putting in $150 per month. If the market's up, well that's great, our existing assets have gone up. If the market's down, we're doing a thing called averaging. Every month by putting money in, we can average it off our returns and it's also a great way for savings.

Managed funds can also be used as a great diversification tool, in that if we say we want to have our money invested, it doesn't have to necessarily be in shares.

We can also invest in International shares and also exposure to another important area, which is commercial property.

Most of us couldn't afford to go buy a commercial property because A, they're very expensive, and B, they can also be a little bit tricky in terms of renting them, because we may not have tenants and so forth.

By investing in managed funds, they have access to assets called property trusts. These can be Australian and International. That gives us exposure to a very important asset sector.

Most of these funds will have prime property in the major cities in Australia, which ordinarily we couldn't get access to.

Most of our Superannuation is invested through these vehicles including Industry and Retail Funds. In selecting Managed Funds we need to consider

1. **Longevity of Funds**
2. **Names and Reputation**
3. **Who are the owners of the Fund e.g. a Bank? And are these vested interests?**
4. **Fees especially if these are performance fees.** These can be nasty as some Managers charge a performance fee if they do well though they don't pay you if they don't perform. Not really fair?
5. **Are there any external fees.** If you are recommended Funds by an adviser they must disclose what fees they receive
6. **Make sure the Funds and recommendations are in line with your Risk Profile**

7. **Make sure you understand the Funds and Sectors you are invested in.** For example if you are looking for growth then fixed interest may not be for you. If you are looking for Capital Security, a high percentage of Shares may not be appropriate. Remember, past performance is not necessarily a guarantee of future performance.

What More Help Planning Your Future?

For Free Instant Access to my Financial Membership Site that has a video walkthrough showcasing a typical financial situation. Let us help you plan for a worry free retirement.

Visit my website:
www.willyoumakeit.com.au

CHAPTER SEVEN

Superannuation

Superannuation

"As far as your personal goals are and what you actually want to do with your life, it should never have to do with the government. You should never depend on the government for your retirement, your financial security, for anything. If you do, you're screwed."

Drew Carey

Simply, this is a serious topic and needs to be written as such.

It began for most of us in 1992, with the introduction of the compulsory 'Superannuation Guarantee'. Since then many of us have only looked forward.

Today some twenty years later most of us have some super, but the question is how long will it last and how do you maximise your return? Well, it's not as great as it used to be.

The government has put limits on how much one can contribute into super. They are however, giving special incentives, particularly for people who are close to retirement.

But superannuation is still the most effective way of investing. Contributions are tax deductible, so we can invest and get a tax deduction for investing money.

Australia is the only country that actually allows people to retire tax free. So when you reach the correct age, you can actually pull out your superannuation either as a lump sum or as a pension tax free!

As an investment adviser, I can say anyone who can retire with superannuation is going to be substantially better off, and anyone who can put money to superannuation should be.

That's a big message I want to send.

Traditionally superannuation has provided excellent returns and has rebounded well after the recent Global Financial Crisis, arguably out-performing other mainstream low risk investments.

As we well know, getting one's head around superannuation legislation is not for the uninitiated, having a relationship with a financial planning adviser makes wading through the jargon simple and helps you understand YOUR affairs.

A good financial adviser provides direction for what is best for you. Below are some of the main features of Superannuation you can discuss with your financial planner.

Contributions are tax deductible

Salary sacrifice can be a highly tax-effective pathway to increase your super savings.

This is an agreement made with your employer to direct (sacrifice) a portion of your salary, wage or income into super or other legal allowances in accordance with the Australian Taxation Office.

This can be a substantial benefit because the money comes from your pre-tax (gross) salary and is taxed at just 15% on its way into your fund, instead of your marginal tax rate, which could be double that.

Interesting fact, the ATO states that before entering any agreement over Salary Sacrificing to consult your financial adviser, another reason why you need one, just in case you're not convinced already!

Most recently co-contributions have been reduced and apply only for low income earners and for a co-contribution of up to $500.00, for example to receive the co-contribution maximum you must inject $1000.00 above a compulsory Superannuation Guarantee.

However every dollar less than the threshold still applies, so it's worth seeking financial advice.

Spouse contributions

Ideal for when a spouse is a low income earner on less than $13,000 per annum in today's terms.

A benefit of a maximum tax offset of $540.00 may apply and is well worth researching with your financial planner to check your eligibility.

Remember too, as governments come and go, so do these legislations.

A financial planner will keep abreast of any changes as they occur, sharing the knowledge with your best interest at heart.

This enabling you to optimise outcomes of these changes just like Josie and Alex, they left it to me!

Imagine having to keep up to date yourself, pouring through legislation, fine print and deciphering the impact.

Un-deducted contributions

So what are un-deducted contributions? This is where you can actually put $180,000 a year of after tax money into super. So you want to ask what is the advantage of putting $180,000 in?

Well, if you were to deposit $180,000 in your personal name in a bank and it is earning interest, well, you're going to pay taxes on marginal rates.

If your marginal rate is more than 15 percent, you're better off putting it into super, especially if you don't need it, as you cannot touch the money until you retire.

You're better off putting it into a superannuation fund where it's earning money at a tax rate of only 15 percent.

There's also huge advantages of having shares in a superannuation fund through dividend imputation credits, whereby if a company is paying tax at 30 percent, the super fund is going to pay tax at 15 percent, the additional difference can actually be claimed through the super fund.

I'm a very big proponent of superannuation.

Super guarantee charge

The whole intention of superannuation today, is the government doesn't want to be funding Australians in their retirement, so they need to use the SGC or superannuation guarantee charge.

It's currently at 9.5 percent and it's going to increase over the next several years.

So what the government is saying is that it's up to us to fund our own retirement, we're not going to help you.

But they're also giving very big incentives for people who do retire on superannuation.

Do you know what they are? If you answered no, you probably need some guidance.

Self-Managed Super Funds

Shares and property as a Super alternative

There has been a huge rise recently of people creating their own self-managed superannuation funds, or SMSFs. The reason why people have been setting up SMSFs are, firstly, they're discontent with fund managers and the fees charged.

Secondly, they think that they can do it better themselves.

Most particularly, with the recent change to government legislation, superannuation funds have been able to do limited gearing or borrowing to buy investment property.

This has actually created a major opportunity for accountants, large investment advisors, property spruikers and so forth.

To me, the opportunity is great because, in theory, if you wanted to pay off a loan on an investment property, you have to pay this with after tax dollars.

So depending upon your marginal tax rates, you have to earn your money, pay your tax and pay off the debt.

By having a loan in a separate fund scenario, and doing it for the right reasons, the money coming into it is separate and is a tax dividend.

Therefore if the money can be used to repay an investment loan you are actually paying off the loan with pretax dollars. There is really no other way to do this. So if done correctly it can be a very effective wealth creation strategy.

However, there's a number of risks associated with this strategy. The first is poor advice.

There has been the creation and growth of many property spruikers selling to trustees of superannuation funds in poor unsuitable areas – overpriced, and with little rental yield, generally resulting in a small capital gain, if any.

The problem that we've got is that the whole idea of having your own superannuation fund is to provide a pension or to fund retirement.

If trustees of funds are being led or steered to buying poor property, this is going to cause major problems and we're not going to see it now. We're going to see it in the next few years when people are retiring.

And if these properties are not going to give a good yield, it is going to create problems, Remember, properties give a very small yield after you pay expenses and so forth, you can't rely on a property to fund a retirement.

It might be good to get capital growth, what you're going to find to fund your retirement, you'll need to eventually sell this property.

If these properties have gone down in value or are in areas with distressed values, in some cases, you can't sell them.

For example house and land packages for sale built in neighbouring areas where there is already an oversupply will be problematic for investors when selling because of competition and lower equity outcomes.

Same applies when buying into larger unit blocks, many experience the same challenges with oversupply, and this can be a very big problem!

I actually foresee that Australia will go through a large litigation process with these types of superannuation funds.

People who have bought these properties are going to go to retire and they're going to find that they can't get an income stream out of these properties that's sufficient to retire on, and what's even worse is they can't sell these properties.

If they do sell the properties, they're going to experience capital losses.

At that point in time, you're going to see real estate agents, advisors, accountants and banks all come under the microscope.

The banks are trying at this point in time to remove their liability by saying that with the superannuation loans, they want the financial planners to sign off on the strategy.

To me, that's a way of saying, well, the banks are already going to see a future problem and they're trying to distance themselves from any litigation. The writing is on the wall.

In terms of property, one of the other things I want to talk about is that there is a lot of restrictions of a member of a fund selling a property to a superannuation fund.

However, there is some allowances for commercial property.

A really good strategy, is for those who run their businesses through a commercial property.

If there is sufficient need, resources, etcetera and circumstances are right , then people can actually sell their business premises into a superannuation fund.

What that will do is actually free up capital, but also give potential future revenue in retirement.

With superannuation funds, there's numerous advantages in buying shares and managed funds through imputation credits on dividends.

There's also the allowance where members can actually sell listed shares into their superannuation fund.

So providing that they do an analysis of capital gains tax that can also be an effective strategy.

I think what people have to remember, is that superannuation is aimed to fund retirement.

By setting up your own superannuation fund as a trustee, you're taking on that responsibility.

If anyone sets up their own superannuation fund, you should understand the risks but also the potential liabilities of being a trustee of your own fund in terms of action that can be taken against you, particularly if these funds are not run correctly, not invested properly and they may actually fail the objective of creating an income in retirement.

Also remember as a Trustee of a Superannuation Fund you must have an Investment strategy which is documented. If you get audited this is usually requested.

Industry Super Funds: The myth

There's a myth out there that the industry funds are a lot better because they charge less fees, and a lot of these are being run by various industry body groups.

There's a real estate industry fund, health industry fund, building industry fund etc.

Now, in a lot of the cases, these funds are good in terms of a certain amount of money, they can be very effective. To dispel some of the myths.

» **Fees.** There's a lot of wholesale funds out there that are very competitive in terms of their fees. I think you've also got to understand that with the industry funds, the reason why they are charging lower fees is they're not paying a lot of staff to actually look after the fund. So the question is, are you in good hands?

» **Quality of investment.** Top fund managers are not working for the industry funds, so there is an argument whether they actually have the best performing fund managers working for them.

» **Valuations.** A lot of the industry funds buy commercial property and they're not valuing those properties in terms of every six months. Frequently when they project the value of their assets, it's based upon commercial property values that may or may not be correct. One could say they are simply providing a product without much due diligence.

» **Expertise.** A lot of fund managers' performance is based on certain information. Many fund managers sell their funds based on past performance every six months, twelve months, five years, and etc. These are all averages and there's no guarantee that what they've done in the past (short or long term) is going to be an indication of future performance.

One thing that is very important to note is that the fund managers are human beings and they're out to obviously do the best for themselves.

What we find is that the fund managers are bouncing around from one fund to another. You might have a brilliant fund manager who creates a great return in your fund, and then the next year he goes to a competitor.

Now, the fund manager is going to use that performance to sell their future investments, not yours.

Historically performance for those funds is now at the competitor's! So it's difficult to make an investment decision based on past performance.

My experience is these guys don't last very long in these funds. The problem is with the advisors, you don't know when they leave, they might have clients invested in a certain fund, and they might be doing okay.

The fund manager, the guy who's responsible for getting the good returns, you may not know for 12 months that they have left, by then it could have some negative returns.

So that's another difficulty of fund managers. The message here is maintain a watchful eye, as I said earlier - know your business!

What More Help Planning Your Future?

For Free Instant Access to my Financial Membership Site that has a video walkthrough showcasing a typical financial situation. Let us help you plan for a worry free retirement.

Visit my website:
www.willyoumakeit.com.au

CHAPTER EIGHT

Getting the insurance you need

Getting the insurance you need

"If a child, a spouse, a life partner, or a parent depends on you and your income, you need life insurance."

Suze Orman

I touched on this in my chapter on superannuation, it's really important you get the right cover. Australians are notoriously under insured, don't become one of them, especially when you can actually afford it.

If you don't know how, this is another area a financial planner has great expertise in, don't leave things to chance.

Generally when I assess the need and amount of Life Insurance required I look at what is the current level of debt and how would this be repaid with the loss of the Primary income earner or spouse.

I also consider:

» Same if there is proposed debt on new acquisitions.
» How many financial dependents and how would they be raised and funded.
» What is the level of income needed in retirement and how would that be affected with the loss of income now required to maintain assets.

Trauma Insurance

This insurance has become quite relevant and essential with the advances in modern medicine. In the "old days" a stroke, heart attack or cancer would generally be the end.

Not so today and with excellent medical attention these are sometimes now just a bump in the road and we are either surviving or living with the conditions for many years.

Trauma Insurance pays a lump sum on the diagnosis of listed conditions such as those above.

It's designed to assist lifestyle and expenditure needs during this period and I believe is essential and worthy of research.

Life and total permanent disability insurance

What is it?

Life Insurance - Designed specifically to assist those left behind in the event of your death to fulfill any financial commitments you may have had.

Total Permanent Disability Insurance - Designed to provide lump sum benefit to the insured in the event of a medically diagnosed injury resulting in the inability to work.

Do I need it?

Imagine the occurrence of an unforeseen event, could you look after yourself or your dependents?

Superannuation is the best way of one funding life and TPD insurance.

If you pay for life insurance and TPD insurance out of your own pocket, you can't claim a tax deduction. If a superannuation fund pays the premiums, it actually can claim a tax deduction.

It now saves you the cash flow and is tax effective, in that contributions go into super before tax. It pays for the premiums, it gets the tax deduction.

There's also conditions of release that need to be understood, it's very important you receive an explanation of how this works.

Income protection through superannuation

What is Income Protection Insurance?

This type of cover insures a predetermined amount of income you will receive in the event of injury or illness, preventing you from being able to work.

Premiums are usually determined based of the coverage and waiting time, it's ideal for sole traders in particular.

Do I need it?

If you are in a high risk industry such as the building game, I would certainly say yes particularly if you are self employed, there are many considerations to weigh up.

In certain respects, I also recommend some people have income protection funded through their super. Income protection should generally be held in one's personal name because:

»   you can get a tax deduction for the premiums and;

» if you do have to and make a claim, you can go straight to the insurance company and you don't have to go through a trustee in a superfund. In cases where people can't afford to pay their income protection, superfunds provide leverage paying for this. I would say, it's better if the superfund pays for an income protection policy and you have an income protection policy, rather than not having an income protection policy that you can't afford to pay for.

What would happen if ....

What would happen to you if yo had a major accident. Maybe your questions would go like this;

» How can I pay the mortgage?
» How can I pay household bills, like food and utilities?
» Then there's the car repayments, how can I manage them?
» How can I pay the school fees?
» How will we live?

What I want you to do is answer questions these questions.

You already know from previous questions, about how much it costs to exist. What you need for a comfortable retirement, right? Do it now, it's important, you never know when your life will change.

Tell me, how did you go? Do you have all the answers? Or do you need some good advice to give you the answers?

I think for most of you, I know the answer, there's no shame, we can't be great at everything, life's busy.

What's important is people need to prioritise, it's most likely you are not a risk taker, unknowingly you are exposing yourself to great risk.

By now you're either on a mission to make change or simply thinking, wow does this guy ramble. If I can impart anything here it is to protect yourself, get good advice and sleep well at night.

Stepped versus Level Premiums

One of the major issues facing this industry is clients don't like paying for insurance premiums. There is the belief that "nothing bad will ever happen to me" or I'd rather invest the premiums then pay "dead money" to an insurance company.

Unfortunately its only when disaster strikes that we really see the true need for insurance.

To alleviate the financial pressures of paying for insurance premiums we can now have our Superannuation funds pay for Term, limited TPD and income protection policies.

When clients ask me what is the cheapest way to pay for premiums it may sound weird though I tell them it's done by paying more up front. This is what "Level Premiums" are.

I always tell my clients that Insurers bet on the probability of something happening to you such as death, illness etc.

They base the premiums on this (as a tip try not to smoke as premiums are double that of nonsmokers – make sense?) Every year as we get older the premiums increase as there is more of a chance that something bad will happen.

This is known as stepped premiums. They are cheap when you first take them out (and usually when we are younger) though as they increase each year they can become very expensive so much that when we really need the coverage we can't afford it.

The alternative is to pay level premiums. These do not increase with age only if you increase the insurance coverage.

They are a bit more to start with - though do not increase over time.

This is the best way to fund long term insurance. Imagine if we were paying the same amount now for our insurance then what we were paying 10 years ago!

That would be fantastic and definitely affordable.

So when I speak to clients particularly my younger clients that require insurance for many years I will always suggest this type of structure.

The numbers show that it's usually after 7 years that they are better off and the savings can be in the tens of thousands of dollars.

For my clients without kids and foresight quite often the best time to get insurance is when we don't need it that is when we are young and healthy.

The odds are that later on we will get a mortgage, have kids and so forth.

So if I can get insurance premiums being paid by a 30 year old for the price a 21 year old is paying I have done my job.

It can get quite expensive as we get older so it's good to get it when you are young and hopefully lock in level premiums.

Key Man Insurance

What is Keyman Insurance?

Simply put it is life insurance taken on the key person in a business. Protecting a company in the event that anything happens to these people. Here are some examples of why you may need this in your business:

» Disability of the key employee which results of an accident or any mishap
» Incapability to work due to prolonged or serious illness
» Death

These events can impact on the business detrimentally causing a void affecting profitability. Generally the company is the primary beneficiary with key person or key man insurance. The premiums are paid for by the business.

In cases where the loss results in the company closure, the proceeds can be used to pay off company liabilities such as debtors, employees, training etc. It can provide cushioning to the business, particularly if the loss is substantial.

As this is applicable to a smaller percentage of my readers it may provide little relevance to most, I really believe though knowledge is king and it's a good thing to be aware of options, as things may change.

What More Help Planning Your Future?

For Free Instant Access to my Financial Membership Site that has a video walkthrough showcasing a typical financial situation. Let us help you plan for a worry free retirement.

Visit my website:
www.willyoumakeit.com.au

CHAPTER NINE

It's never too late! or too early!

It's never too late! Or too early!

"My father used to say that it's never too late to do anything you wanted to do. And he said, 'You never know what you can accomplish until you try.'"

Michael Jordan

It's never too early or too late to seek the advice of a financial planner!

So let's relate the financial planning process back to the 6 steps of financial freedom. When I see a client for the first time I'll do an intensive fact finding mission.

This will get as much factual information as I can but also get a feel for what my clients risk profile and asset preference and comfort zone.

The key is to have the client prepare as much information before the meeting so we can be productive as possible. There is nothing worse than asking a client questions only to hear " I don't know – I'll have to get back to you"

I will ask clients to bring information such as:

- » Details of Assets and Liabilities
- » Details of their Superannuation
- » Details of any Insurances held
- » A Risk profile questionnaire

All of this enables us to go over the concepts of financial planning and in most cases identifies inefficiencies in the client' strategies.

Then we get into the interesting stuff where I would ask a client as to why they think there are inefficiencies?

Most often they won't know so I put it like this: In all our working lives we are forced to plan. We work on budgets and forecasts and targets.

So in effect we all need to plan for our employers but how many of us actually plan for ourselves – that's where I say inefficiencies arise – it's due to a lack of planning.

And that's where a good financial planner will help. By setting up a Financial Plan.

Once we have the Plan and everybody understands the how, what, why, when and importantly how much then we can look at products.

Unfortunately most Australians historically have been product orientated that is they will invest in a fund, buy a property, get Super and (hopefully) insurance.

Usually they are dealing with several different providers and usually they have their own interests and they definitely don't coordinate with each other.

How often will the bank manager or mortgage broker speak to the Super adviser or the Insurance adviser to ensure all matters are thought of.

So we need to ask: "But are those products right?"

I always say put the horse before the cart. If we have a strategy or plan in place the products will always fall into place.

It's then up to the clients and the Planner to work together to implement the plan and incorporate the products in a timely and effective manner.

Once the plan is up and working we need to ensure proper records are kept. This will be for both short term such as providing information to the Accountant but also long term.

I can't stress the importance of the client maintaining good long term records and not simply relying on the Planner.

In the event of say a death or injury (to either the client or planner), the partner should have ease of access to all documents and what has happened.

In other words we need to protect against all contingencies so it all keeps on moving.

The last stage is that of review. A Financial plan done today will not last forever. Things change – circumstances, career, family and we always need to be able to adapt.

It's so important to carry out periodical reviews to make sure we stay on track.

The final thing we need to do is to cost out this process. We need to make sure all fees, commissions and ongoing charges are up front and transparent.

Sure we can do well for a client but as with everything there has to be value for the client dollar wise.

We need to ensure we have the client's trust so putting everything on the table up front is the only way to go.

Albert Einstein famously quoted on his definition of insanity: "doing the same thing over again and expecting a different result". So start planning!

Summing Up

Here's a handy check list to help you on your way

» Do you need more money in retirement?
» Are you worried about your financial future?
» Are you getting the best returns on your investments?
» Would you like advice and someone with expert knowledge?
» Would you like access to taxation advice tailored for your circumstances?
» Do you need unbiased advice on superannuation, shares, property, and managed funds?
» Do you seek excellence in service and a qualified practitioner?
» Are you happy to pay for good advice, but can't find it?

Alex and Josie Fast Forward

Alex and Josie are now in their 60s. Over the last 20 years they have acquired 2 more Investment properties, one in their personal name and one in their Superannuation portfolio.

They have been salary sacrificing into their Super fund so that the debt on the property has been repaid and they now have a tidy sum in their Super.

They plan on retiring at age 65. Our strategy will be to sell the Investment property in their personal name and repay the balance of their small home mortgage.

They have also recently received a small inheritance from Josie's Mother.

After the little renovation, overseas holiday and purchase of a new car there will be a nice sum left over. We plan to keep a sum of cash available and place a nice lump sum into Super as an Undeducted Contribution.

When they reach 65 we will convert the Super to a Pension Fund and then sell the property (tax free!!!). They will then have the luxury of a Super fund with Lots of cash.

A new Financial Plan will be done showing them how to invest these funds.

At this stage of their Financial Lives they require a solid return whilst not taking too much risk as confirmed by their new risk profile. We need to make sure there is enough liquidity to support the monthly withdrawal of their pensions.

This will be done as a combination of Fixed Interest and moderate growth assets.

We will also make sure we maximise any of their entitlement to Social Security.

These funds need to last a long time and hopefully there will still be an estate to leave to their kids.

Hopefully it will be smooth sailing from here.

Taking Control

I have touched on this subject briefly.

Having a Financial Planner is a valuable asset, assisting in preparation of a solid financial plan along with its implementation, generally things you can't do yourself.

I can't stress enough, the importance of all clients taking control and being responsible for their future, the need to know exactly what is happening and why.

Good record keeping is paramount, not to mention the savings to be had at taxation time, as accountants charge by the hour and well prepared records will represent a significant saving and avoid frustration.

When you receive statements from Fund Managers, Insurers and so forth, take time to read and if needed contact the adviser to discuss.

Markets can fall and you need to understand the implications of say selling in a fallen market or conversely of holding on. The same applies to a rising market.

If you have a rental property keep a folder. I prefer to keep separate sections:

Rental Statements

1. Copies of all expenses such as Rates, Repairs and so forth
2. Mortgage statements
3. Details of the purchase including Solicitor purchase statement and all costs associated with Purchase including the Quantity Surveyor report. This will assist in calculating future capital gains on sale.
4. Details of the Mortgage.

If you own shares I recommend a folder. I prefer to keep separate sections:

1. Copies of all Dividend statements
2. Separate section for each share acquired

» Copies of contract note
» Copies of any dividends reinvested
» Copies of any further acquisitions
» Copies of contract notes for sale

Most importantly, never be shy to pick up the phone or send your Planner an email. We are there to help and if we don't hear we think things are ok.

A good Planner should notify you as new opportunities arise, outside the scheduled review time. As I said Planners are there to help though this should be a "partnership".

Working together will ensure you reach your goals.

So who ticks all the boxes?

When Josie and Alex came to me they had many questions and few answers, you may very well feel the same way.

If you want to change your financial position, enter the investment property market, set some goals so you will make it! The answer is MASU Group, that means flexibility and diversity, what you want, not what we want.

Tailor made, for you, not just focused on products we want to sell you, it's your choice. Trust is the most essential ingredient and here's where MASU Group can help.

We are a boutique agency with a team of experienced industry professionals, dedicated in providing premium advice and winning outcomes for our clients. Our goal is for you to enjoy an optimistic, stress free life at any age, a little help from us can make a big difference.

Getting in Touch

The talented team at MASU Group may at some time lend their expertise to your portfolio to provide you with the best outcome.

Heading up the financial planning arm of MASU Group, I'm also a Director so you can rest assured the buck stops with me.

With over 25 years industry experience with qualifications in Accounting, Financial Planning, Real Estate and Mortgage lending, I provide a holistic, educated advice, just what YOU need.

To meet the rest of our friendly team visit www.MASU.com.au today.

The MASU Group offer the following services:

» Financial planning
» Wealth creation
» Superannuation
» Tax planning
» Life insurance
» Property
» Residential & Commercial Mortgage
» Shares and Equity Investment
» Mortgage and Debt Structuring
» Budgeting and overall financial management

We only provide recommendations after considering your individual objectives, financial situation and needs.

We also offer ongoing monitoring of your portfolio.

The MASU Group are proud of their transparency, we will provide you with full disclosure on how we operate to give you the peace of mind you deserve, things like our fee structure, commissions and trailers, there are no secrets, just ask us.

Visit our website and you'll find the answers www.MASU.com.au

No matter, who you are or whatever your circumstance, it's time to start planning or to review your situation, life's what you make of it.

Remember it's never too late, or too early!

My goal is to set you on a path, a path to financial freedom, comfortable retirement and a life free from the stress of financial struggle.

The MASU team are experienced financial planners and industry professionals. The company established in 1995 has now grown to a team of experienced planners throughout Australia, we love what we do and you will too!

Find out more about MASU Group, visit us at MASUgroup.com.au or call us today on 1300 786 903 for a complimentary financial assessment and get your future on track!

You have the right to ask us about our charges, the type of advice we will give you, and what you can do if you have a complaint about our services.

Key information is available on our website. If you need more information or clarification, please ask us.

Book Bonuses

Please register this book at www.willyoumakeit.com.au to receive complimentary access to the bonus videos that covers our initial discussions with my clients.

I go over how to plan for your retirement and how to invest for your future in this interactive session.

What More Help Planning Your Future?

For Free Instant Access to my Financial Membership Site that has a video walkthrough showcasing a typical financial situation. Let us help you plan for a worry free retirement.

Visit my website:
www.willyoumakeit.com.au